VICE PRESIDENT

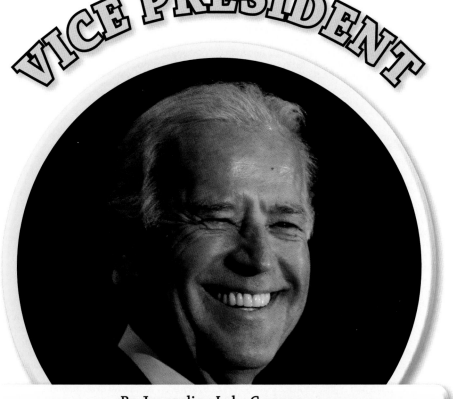

By Jacqueline Laks Gorman
Reading consultant: Susan Nations, M.Ed.,
author/literacy coach/consultant in literacy development

WEEKLY READER®

PUBLISHING

Please visit our web site at www.garethstevens.com
For a free color catalog describing our list of high-quality books,
call 1-800-542-2595 (USA) or 1-800-387-3178 (Canada). Our fax: 1-877-542-2596

Library of Congress Cataloging-in-Publication Data
Gorman, Jacqueline Laks, 1955–
   Vice president / by Jacqueline Laks Gorman.
      p. cm. — (Know your government)
   Includes bibliographical references and index.
   ISBN-10: 1-4339-0096-3   ISBN-13: 978-1-4339-0096-9 (lib. bdg.)
   ISBN-10: 1-4339-0124-2   ISBN-13: 978-1-4339-0124-9 (soft cover)
   1. Vice-Presidents—United States—Juvenile literature. I. Title.
   JK609.5.G674   2008
   352.23'90973—dc22   2008042490

This edition first published in 2009 by
Weekly Reader® Books
An Imprint of Gareth Stevens Publishing
1 Reader's Digest Road
Pleasantville, NY 10570-7000 USA

Copyright © 2009 by Gareth Stevens, Inc.

Executive Managing Editor: Lisa M. Herrington
Editors: Brian Fitzgerald and Barbara Kiely Miller
Creative Director: Lisa Donovan
Senior Designer: Keith Plechaty
Photo Researchers: Charlene Pinckney and Diane Laska-Swanke
Publisher: Keith Garton

Photo credits: cover & title page © Eric Thayer/Reuters/Corbis; p. 5 Ted S. Warren/AP; p. 6 © Ed Clark/Time & Life Pictures/Getty Images; p. 7 AP; p. 9 Tim Sloan/Reuters/Landov/Pool; p. 10 Pablo Martinez Monsivais/AP; p. 11 Neal Ulevich/AP; p. 13 Jae C. Hong/AP; p. 14 Rick Wilking/AP/Pool; p. 15 Paul Sancya/AP; p. 17 © North Wind Picture Archives; p. 18 © Hulton Archive/Getty Images; p. 19 Lyndon B. Johnson Library Photo by Cecil Stoughton; p. 20 © Thomas D. Mcavoy/Time & Life Pictures/Getty Images; p. 21 Paramount Pictures.

Printed in the United States of America

1 2 3 4 5 6 7 8 9 10 09 08

Cover Photo: Joseph Biden was elected vice president of the United States in 2008.

TABLE OF CONTENTS

Words that appear in the glossary are printed in
boldface type the first time they appear in the text.

CHAPTER 1

Who Is the Vice President?

The vice president of the United States is an important leader. The vice president is the second highest-ranking person in the government. The vice president works closely with the president.

In 2008, Joseph Biden was elected vice president.

The vice president helps the president decide the best way to run the country. The vice president and the president are the only leaders **elected**, or chosen, by the whole country.

Washington, D.C., is the capital of the United States. It is the center of the U.S. government. The vice president lives and works there. The vice president works in the White House.

President Dwight D. Eisenhower (left) often met with his vice president, Richard Nixon (right). They were in office from 1953 to 1961. Nixon became president in 1968.

The address of the vice president's home is Number One Observatory Circle in Washington, D.C.

The vice president's house is on the grounds of the U.S. Naval Observatory. Trained guards called the Secret Service protect the vice president.

The president travels on a plane called *Air Force One*. The vice president's plane is called *Air Force Two*.

CHAPTER 2

What Does the Vice President Do?

The law gives the vice president only two duties. The first duty is more important. The vice president must be ready for the top job in the country. The president may get sick or die. He may also quit. If that happens, the vice president takes over.

The vice president's second duty is important, too. The **Senate** is part of Congress. Congress is the group that makes the country's laws. The vice president is the leader of the Senate. The vice president does not usually vote in the Senate. If there is a tie, the vice president votes to break it.

As vice president, Dick Cheney (left) listened when President George W. Bush spoke to Congress.

9

Vice President Dick Cheney joined President George W. Bush and members of the Cabinet for a meeting in July 2007.

The vice president is a member of the **Cabinet**. People in the Cabinet are the president's top helpers. Cabinet members work in education, health, and other important areas. The Cabinet meets with the president to talk about ways to fix problems.

The president also asks the vice president to do other things. Sometimes, the vice president leads groups that study problems and come up with answers. The vice president travels around the world to meet with other leaders, too.

George H.W. Bush was vice president from 1981 to 1989. He visited China in 1985. Bush was later elected president.

CHAPTER 3

How Does a Person Become Vice President?

To become vice president, a person must be at least 35 years old. He or she must be a **citizen** born in the United States. He or she must have lived in the United States for at least 14 years.

The vice president and the president are **running mates**. They are a team. Voters elect the president and vice president every four years.

Many people have the same ideas about running the country. They belong to groups called **political parties**. The two main political parties are the Democratic Party and the Republican Party. The parties pick **candidates** for president and vice president.

The Republican Party picked John McCain (left) and Sarah Palin (right) as its candidates for president and vice president in 2008.

The candidates travel across the country. They talk to voters and give speeches. They explain how they would run the country. They have **debates** with each other about important issues.

Joseph Biden (left) and Sarah Palin (right) had a debate when they were running for vice president in 2008.

In 2008, Election Day was November 4. Joseph Biden and Barack Obama were elected vice president and president.

Election Day is in November. People all over the country vote. They pick the candidates who they want to lead the country. In January, the new president and vice president take over.

CHAPTER 4

Famous Vice Presidents

Many vice presidents have become part of history. Several went on to become president. Some took over when the president could not finish the job. Others ran in elections and won.

In 1789, John Adams became the first vice president. He served under George Washington for a little more than eight years. Adams was elected president himself in 1796.

John Adams was the United States' first vice president. He was also the second president.

Vice President Aaron Burr shot and killed Alexander Hamilton in a duel in 1804.

One vice president is famous for doing the wrong thing. Aaron Burr became vice president in 1801. He argued with Alexander Hamilton, an important leader who helped to shape the country. Burr and Hamilton had a **duel**. Burr killed Hamilton but did not go to jail. He finished his job as vice president!

In 1841, President William Henry Harrison died. John Tyler was the vice president. He was the first vice president to take over after a president died. That has happened seven times since then.

Vice President Lyndon Johnson was sworn in as the new president after John F. Kennedy was killed in 1963.

Harry Truman was the vice president in 1945. The United States was fighting World War II. President Franklin D. Roosevelt died that year. Truman became the new president. He worked hard to help the country win the war. Truman ran for president in the next election and won.

Vice President Harry Truman (left) became president after Franklin D. Roosevelt (right) died in 1945.

Some vice presidents became more famous after they left office. Al Gore was vice president under President Bill Clinton. In 2000, Gore ran for president against George W. Bush. Gore lost a close election.

Gore has worked to help protect the environment. In 2007, he won an important award, the Nobel Peace Prize, for his work.

Al Gore gives speeches about ways people can help the environment.

Glossary

Cabinet: a group of people who lead government departments. Cabinet members work for the president.

candidates: people who are running for office

citizen: an official member of a country who has certain rights, such as voting

debates: formal arguments between candidates about where they stand on important issues

duel: a fight with set rules between two people who use guns or swords

elected: chosen by people who voted

political parties: groups of people who have similar beliefs and ideas

running mates: people who run together for president and vice president

Senate: one of the two parts of Congress. The other part is the House of Representatives.

To Find Out More

Books

How Is a Government Elected? Your Guide to Government (series). Baron Bedeksy (Crabtree, 2008)

What's a President and Vice President? First Guide to Government (series). Nancy Harris (Heinemann, 2007)

Web Sites

Ben's Guide to U.S. Government for Kids
bensguide.gpo.gov
This site is a guide to the national government, including the vice presidency.

Children's Biography of the Vice President
www.whitehouse.gov/kids/vicepresident
Learn all about the vice president, and take a tour of the vice president's office.

Index

About the Author

Jacqueline Laks Gorman is a writer and an editor. She grew up in New York City. She has worked on many kinds of books and has written several children's series. She lives with her husband, David, and children, Colin and Caitlin, in DeKalb, Illinois. She registered to vote when she turned 18 and votes in every election.